TODAY'S SUPERSTARS
Sports

Dale
EARNHARDT, JR.

by Geoffrey M. Horn

GARETH**STEVENS**
GS
P U B L I S H I N G
A Member of the WRC Media Family of Companies

Please visit our web site at: www.garethstevens.com
For a free color catalog describing Gareth Stevens Publishing's
list of high-quality books and multimedia programs, call
1-800-542-2595 (USA) or 1-800-387-3178 (Canada).
Gareth Stevens Publishing's fax: (414) 332-3567.

Library of Congress Cataloging-in-Publication Data

Horn, Geoffrey M.
    Dale Earnhardt, Jr. / by Geoffrey M. Horn.
      p. cm. — (Today's superstars: sports)
    Includes bibliographical references and index.
    ISBN 0-8368-6182-5 (lib. bdg.)
    1. Earnhardt, Dale, Jr.—Juvenile literature. 2. Stock car drivers—
United States—Biography—Juvenile literature. I. Title.
GV1032.E18H67   2006
796.72092—dc22   2005032078

Updated and reprinted in 2006.

This edition first published in 2006 by
Gareth Stevens Publishing
A Member of the WRC Media Family of Companies
330 West Olive Street, Suite 100
Milwaukee, WI 53212 USA

This edition copyright © 2006 by Gareth Stevens, Inc.

Editor: Jim Mezzanotte
Art direction and design: Tammy West
Picture research: Diane Laska-Swanke

Photo credits: Cover, pp. 7, 8, 11, 12, 14, 19, 20, 22, 24, 25,
27 © AP/Wide World Photos; p. 17 © Peter Carvelli/Getty Images;
p. 28 © Scott Boehm/Getty Images

Printed in the United States of America

2 3 4 5 6 7 8 9 10 09 08 07 06

CONTENTS

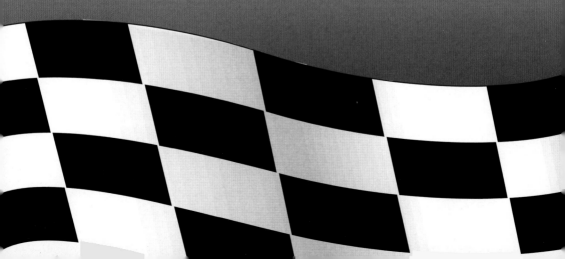

DAYTONA

Many races are run at Daytona International Speedway. But each year, there's only one Daytona 500. Some people call it the Great American Race. Every February, the best NASCAR drivers test their skills and cars on the Florida track. For Dale Earnhardt, Jr., the Daytona 500 is more than just a race. It's a matter of life and death.

A Win for the Intimidator

The Daytona 500 had always been a jinxed race for Dale's dad. Dale Earnhardt, Sr., was a NASCAR legend. He was called "The Intimidator" because of his fearless racing style. He had won other races at Daytona. But for two decades, he had failed to win the biggest race of all.

Before 1998, he had entered the Daytona 500 nineteen times. Seventeen times he led the pack. He even led twice in the final lap.

But each time he had come away empty-handed. "I've said before that those things didn't bother me," he told reporters. "I lied. You don't come that close to winning the Daytona 500 and not feel it. It hurt."

His years of waiting ended on Sunday, February 15, 1998. This time, his black Chevy with the big number 3 led for the last sixty-one laps. A crowd of 185,000 roared with excitement as the race ended. "We won it! We won it! We won it!" he shouted as he got out of his car. Other drivers and their crew members rushed to congratulate him. It was one of racing's most moving moments.

Death in the Afternoon

In 2001, the Daytona 500 began with cheers and ended in horror. For most of the day, fans had seen some thrilling action on the track. The leaders were tightly bunched.

FACT FILE

In 1959, the prize money for the Daytona 500 totaled $19,050. Today, about $1.5 million in prize money is up for grabs.

On the final lap, Michael Waltrip was in first place, and Dale Jr. was in second place. Behind them, Dale Sr.'s black Chevy was fighting for third. Suddenly, a bump from another car sent Dale Sr.'s car off course. As his car crashed into a wall, Kenny Schrader's car plowed into it. Schrader walked away from the accident. Earnhardt didn't.

An ambulance rushed Dale Sr. to the hospital. Doctors tried to revive him, but nothing worked. The end came at 5:16 P.M. on Sunday, February 18. The Intimidator was dead.

More than 200,000 fans at the Daytona Speedway saw the accident. So did millions of people watching the race on television. Dale Jr. was one of the few who didn't see the crash as it happened. He was ahead of his father's car, fighting for the lead.

FACT FILE

During his career, the Intimidator earned more than $28 million in prize money. He made 676 starts in major races. He won 76 of them, and he finished in the top five 281 times.

Another Earnhardt Wins

Dale Jr. returned to the Daytona Speedway in July 2001, winning the Pepsi 400 less than five months after his father's death. His emotions overwhelmed him. "I can't imagine it," he said. "I can't imagine it. I can't sit here and understand it. It makes no sense to me. I can't believe it's happening to me. I don't know why it's happening to me. I just have to stay close to my friends,

Dale Jr. finished first and Michael Waltrip second in the Pepsi 400 at Daytona in July 2001.

7

Need for Speed

Auto racing in the Daytona area began more than a hundred years ago. Since 1903, cars have been running timed races on the smooth, hard-packed sand of Ormond Beach. Today, the heart of the Daytona area is a city called Daytona Beach. About 64,000 people live in the city year round. Millions more come to visit.

The National Association for Stock Car Auto Racing, or NASCAR, began here in 1948. At first, "stock cars" were similar to cars used in everyday driving. Today, the top stock cars are specially made for racing. They are only similar to regular cars on the outside. These cars race at speeds of up to 200 miles (322 kilometers) per hour.

The first NASCAR races in Daytona were held on the beach and along a strip of highway. Then, in 1959, the Daytona International Speedway opened. The Daytona 500 began the same year. As you might guess, the race is 500 miles (805 km) long. The track is almost oval-shaped, and it is 2.5 miles (4 km) long. Each trip around the track is called a lap. A race car needs to complete two hundred laps to finish the Daytona 500.

After winning the Daytona 500 for the first time, Dale Jr. enjoys his moment of glory in Victory Lane.

the people who make me feel good, and maybe I'll figure it out."

He had to wait awhile to win his first Daytona 500. In 2002, a blown tire forced him to make a pit stop. He finished thirty-sixth. After a breakdown early in the 2003 race, the best he could do was twenty-ninth.

Finally, on February 15, 2004 — exactly six years after his father's win — Junior had his own moment in Victory Lane. He charged into the lead with nineteen laps to go. No one could catch him.

After Junior won his first Daytona 500, reporters kept asking him whether he thought he was as good as his dad. He said he wished people would stop making comparisons. "The biggest compliment you can give me is that I remind you of my dad," he said. "But when is the day going to come when I don't have to reflect back? When will I stand on my own merit?"

FACT FILE

Dale Sr. owned race cars as well as raced them. Both Dale Jr. and Michael Waltrip were driving his cars in the race in which he died.

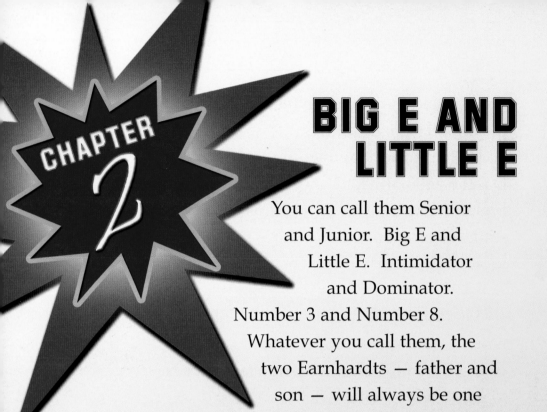

CHAPTER 2

BIG E AND LITTLE E

You can call them Senior and Junior. Big E and Little E. Intimidator and Dominator. Number 3 and Number 8. Whatever you call them, the two Earnhardts — father and son — will always be one of the great stories in racing.

Life in the Fast Lane

Ralph Dale Earnhardt, Sr., grew up in Kannapolis, North Carolina. He dropped out of school in the ninth grade. "I wanted to race — that's all I ever wanted to do," he said. "I didn't care about work or school or anything.

FACT FILE

Today, about 40,000 people live in Kannapolis, which is located near Charlotte. In 2002, the city put up a large statue to honor Dale Sr. In another salute to Number 3, the city's minor league baseball team is called the Kannapolis Intimidators.

All I wanted to do was work on race cars
and then drive race cars. It was always my
dream. ... I was just fortunate enough to be
able to live out that dream."

Big E said that when he was in his late
teens and twenties, he was "wild and crazy,
young and dumb." He was married twice
before he turned twenty-one. Both marriages

This photo of Big E and Little E was
taken at the Daytona Speedway,
nine days before Dale Sr.'s death.

Junior and his older sister Kelley were close friends while they were growing up. Like her brothers, Kelley tried her hand at racing, driving late-model stock cars.

ended in divorce. In 1968, he married Latane Brown. They had a son, Kerry, who was born in 1969. After breaking up with Latane, Big E married Brenda Gee in 1971. A year later, the couple had a daughter, Kelley.

FACT FILE

Ralph Earnhardt — father of Big E and grandfather of Little E — was also a champion race car driver. His nickname was Ironheart. He died in 1973, at the age of forty-five. In 1998, NASCAR named him one of the fifty greatest drivers of all time.

On October 10, 1974, Big E and Brenda had another child — a boy. They named him Ralph Dale Earnhardt, Jr.

Keeping His Distance

Dale Jr. — Little E — was born in the town of Concord, North Carolina. It is located northeast of Charlotte, in the western part of the state. When Little E was very young, his parents separated. He and his sister Kelley lived with Brenda until he was about six years old. Then, their house caught fire and burned to the ground. With no house to live in, Brenda decided she could no longer take care of the kids. She moved away, and she sent Little E and Kelley to live with their father.

In 1982, Big E got married again. His third wife was Teresa Houston. They had

FACT FILE

Dale Jr.'s mother had her own NASCAR connection. Brenda Gee's father, Robert Gee, was a well-known race-car builder.

It Runs in the Family

The Earnhardts aren't the only family with a long NASCAR tradition. Lee Petty was a NASCAR founder. He also won the first Daytona 500. His son, Richard Petty, won the Daytona 500 a record seven times. Richard Petty's nickname was "The King." He had two hundred career wins, with seven NASCAR titles. Richard's son, Kyle Petty, has earned more than $3 million as a NASCAR driver. Adam Petty — Kyle's son — also entered the family business. But he was killed in a crash in 2000.

The Allisons are another leading NASCAR family. In 1998, NASCAR named Bobby Allison one of the fifty greatest drivers of all time. He won the Daytona 500 three times. His brother, Donnie Allison, was a top driver, too. Bobby's son, Davey Allison, was NASCAR's Rookie of the Year in 1987. He won nineteen major races, including the Daytona 500. Davey died in a helicopter accident in 1993.

The Labonte brothers have been NASCAR winners for many years. Terry Labonte was NASCAR champion in 1984 and 1996. His younger brother, Bobby, won the NASCAR championship in 2000. Bobby has earned more than $4 million in his racing career.

Teresa Earnhardt announces a concert at Daytona to honor Dale Sr.'s memory.

known each other since 1978, when they met at a racetrack in Martinsville, Virginia. Teresa was familiar with the NASCAR world. Her father, Hal Houston, raced stock cars. Her uncle, Tommy Houston, won more than $1.5 million as a driver. Because Big E was away a lot, Teresa did most of the child raising.

Dale Jr. still calls his dad his hero. But while he was growing up, he and his father had problems. "We'd go upstairs and sit down on the couch, and he'd be sitting there watching TV in the recliner," Dale Jr. told a reporter for *Rolling Stone* magazine. "You ask him a question and he wouldn't hear you. You rarely even got a response sometimes. He was so in his racing thing, you could hardly sometimes have a conversation with him."

FACT FILE

Teresa and her husband, Dale Sr., built Dale Earnhardt Inc. (DEI) into one of NASCAR's most successful businesses. They had a daughter, Taylor, in 1988. Teresa became a widow when Dale Sr. died at Daytona in 2001. She remains the head of DEI.

RACING
REBEL

Dale Jr. didn't start out to be a race car driver. His older sister Kelley remembers him as being small and shy. "People always walked over him and didn't treat him with respect," she told the *Sporting News*. When Dale Jr. needed money, or just needed to talk to someone, he usually turned to Kelley.

Rocking His World

"Up until I was fourteen or fifteen I was real short," Dale Jr. says. "I wore Wranglers and cowboy hats and fished and raced round on boats and listened to country music."

The world of NASCAR has roots in the rural South, where the "country" lifestyle rules. Many drivers learned their skills on the narrow, twisty mountain roads of western Virginia and North Carolina. They went to country schools in country towns. Where they lived, the radio usually played country music.

It was a big deal, Dale Jr. recalls, when he discovered MTV. "I was a junior [in high school] and I went to a buddy's house and this song came on MTV," he told *Rolling Stone*. The song was "Smells Like Teen Spirit," by Nirvana. "It fit my emotions," he said. "I was tired of listening to my parents. I was tired of living at home. I didn't know what I was gonna do. I didn't have any direction." He was moved by Kurt Cobain's vocal. "The fact that he could sit there and scream into that mike like that gave you a sense of relief."

By 1998, Junior was a top driver in NASCAR's Busch Series.

Taking the Wheel

Kelley told the *Sporting News* that she was more of a daredevil than her brother when she was growing up. "As a teenager," she said, "I didn't think Dale Jr. would be a racer." She remembered him spending a lot of time playing with Matchbox cars. But Dale Jr. wasn't aggressive. He didn't take risks.

In his late teens, the wannabe rebel went to Mitchell Community College in Statesville, North Carolina. He learned about cars and how to fix them. Then, he worked at his father's auto dealership. "I got to where I could do an oil change in eight minutes," he said. "I was really proud of that. People were comin' in there like, man, I want this dude to change my oil."

In his spare time, Dale Jr. started to race stock cars. At first, he drove on

FACT FILE

Dale Earnhardt, Jr., is 6 feet (1.8 meters) tall. He weighs 175 pounds (79 kilograms). On his Web site, he lists his favorite musicians as the Matthew Good Band, Third Eye Blind, Elvis, and Ludacris. He has appeared in music videos for Sheryl Crow and 3 Doors Down.

The Garage Mahal

Hundreds of years ago, Shah Jahan, the emperor of India, was married to a woman named Mumtaz. When she died in 1631, he built a beautiful tomb in her honor. The tomb is called the Taj Mahal. It is one of the world's great treasures.

Today, the world has another building with Mahal in its name. It's located in Mooresville, North Carolina. The place is so big and fancy that it's jokingly called the Garage Mahal. The Garage Mahal holds the head offices of Dale Earnhardt Inc. It also holds a museum. One of the museum's displays is the car Dale Jr. used to win the 2004 Daytona 500. The museum also has Dale Sr.'s NASCAR championship trophies. In addition, there's a shop filled with stuff to buy. Fans from all around the world travel to the Garage Mahal to pay tribute to their NASCAR heroes, Big E and Little E.

Visitors to the Garage Mahal can see the same car Dale Jr. drove to victory at the Daytona 500 in 2004.

small tracks in front of small crowds. "I was having fun driving late-model cars, just messing around," he says. Then, he began getting advice from his uncle, Tony Eury, Sr. Eury remembers Dale Sr. asking him in 1995 if he could help turn Dale Jr. into a driver.

A year later, Junior began driving in the Busch Series. In this NASCAR series, drivers compete in cars that are slightly less powerful than the top NASCAR racing cars. "When I started running Busch, I got serious," he says. How does he explain the change in attitude? "I was seeking my father's approval. I wanted to make him proud. I'd been trying to do that all my life."

Tony Eury, Jr. (left), is Dale Jr.'s cousin. He has been a key member of the Earnhardt racing team.

FAST START

Dale Jr. began entering Busch Series races in 1996. Two years later, in 1998, he won the championship. He led the other drivers with seven wins and 6,055 points. He won the championship again in 1999, with six wins and 6,231 points. His track success in 1998 and 1999 earned him more than $3 million.

Winston Cup Win

In the 1999 racing season, Junior made the jump to the Winston Cup, the top series in NASCAR. He didn't have to wait long to reach the victory circle. On April 2, 2000, Dale Jr. won the DirecTV 500 at the Texas Motor Speedway in Fort Worth. It was only his twelfth Winston Cup race.

In his book *Driver #8*, Dale Jr. describes what it felt like to come in first: "On the

Points for the Championship

In the Busch Series and Nextel Cup (previously called the Winston Cup), the championship is based on points. The winner of each NASCAR race gets at least 180 points. The second-place finisher gets 170 points. For all other drivers, the lower the finish, the fewer the number of points awarded. Drivers can improve their score by earning bonus points. They earn five bonus points, for example, for each lap they are in the lead of a race. Another five-point bonus is given to the driver who leads the most laps in a race.

Earnhardt has been a frequent winner at Talladega Superspeedway. This photo shows him in Talladega's Victory Lane in April 2003.

last lap, I'm so excited, and I can see the
fans are excited as well. When I drive
through Turn 4, I see all of the flashbulbs
flashing. I can't believe it — the people
are screaming and cheering and waving
their arms and hats and … I can't believe
it! We have won a Winston Cup race!"

Making His Points

The year 2000 was Dale Jr.'s first full
season racing in the Winston Cup. He
finished sixteenth in the standings, with
3,516 points. (Dale Sr. had 4,865 points
that year, coming in second behind Bobby
Labonte.) In 2001, the year Big E died,
Little E moved up to eighth place in the
Cup standings. He slipped a bit in 2002,
although he managed two wins and
eleven top-five finishes. Junior had his
best season overall in 2003. That year, he

FACT FILE

One racetrack where Dale Jr. does very well is the Talladega
Superspeedway in Alabama. He won five major races at Talladega
between 2001 and 2004.

Women in NASCAR

Teresa Earnhardt holds a powerful post as head of Dale Earnhardt Inc. But on the track and in the pits, men still rule. Some people think NASCAR would have even more fans if it had more women driving in its races.

Nothing in NASCAR's rules bars a female driver from competing. In the early days of NASCAR, Louise Smith was a well-known racer. In 1977, Janet Guthrie became the first woman to claim a starting spot in the Daytona 500. She came in twelfth and was the top rookie finisher. Today, hopes for a female NASCAR champion may ride with Erin Crocker. Erin began competing in Busch Series events in 2005.

Teresa Earnhardt and her stepson celebrate his first-place finish in the EAS/GNC Live Well 300 at Daytona in February 2002.

Dale Jr. had a narrow escape after he crashed his Corvette C5-R on a test run in California.

ranked third, behind Matt Kenseth and Jimmie Johnson.

The Winston Cup became the Nextel Cup in 2004. Dale Jr. had another fine year. He was fifth in the final standings, only 138 points behind the leader, Kurt Busch. He came up big in some of the biggest races, including the Daytona 500. He was the top money winner, earning $7.2 million. In addition, his sixteen top-five finishes in thirty-six starts were right up there with NASCAR's best.

RISKS AND REWARDS

More than most people, Dale Jr. knows the risks of driving a car at dizzying speeds. After all, his own father died while racing. In July 2004, Junior had a brush with death on a racetrack in California. He lost control of a Corvette he was testing. The car crashed and caught fire. Flames leaped as high as 30 feet (9 m). Junior escaped with burns on his legs and face.

Fan Favorite

Dale Jr. is well paid for the risks he runs. On NASCAR tracks, he has won more

FACT FILE

Each year, fans spend about $1.2 billion on official NASCAR-licensed goods. Items related to Dale Jr., Dale Sr., and racer Jeff Gordon are among the top sellers.

In the Pits

No race car driver can do it all. Every driver needs a
pit crew. During a pit stop, the crew must gas up the
car, change the tires, and try to fix anything that's
broken. A finely tuned crew can save valuable time.
A poorly trained crew can turn a leader into a loser.

Two important jobs on the racing team are the
crew chief and the car chief. The crew chief is in
charge of everything the team does, both in the shop
and in the pit. The car chief makes sure that all the
changes the crew chief orders for the car are actually
carried out. For years, Dale Jr.'s crew chief was his
uncle, Tony Eury, Sr. His car chief was Eury's son,
Tony Jr.

After the 2004 season, Dale Jr. got a new crew chief
and car chief. But things didn't work out. "They really
just couldn't communicate," says Tony Jr. "It's hard to
communicate with Dale Jr. He's not the easiest person
to talk to during a race. That's where stuff started
going downhill."

When the 2005 season started badly,
Earnhardt made big changes in his pit crew.

than $30 million. A long-term deal with Budweiser means he does not have to worry about where his next meal — or beer — is coming from.

Dale Jr. had a tough year in 2005. His points were down, and so were his wins. In his first thirty-two starts, he had only one victory, the USG Sheetrock 400. The pressure on him is intense. NASCAR has a lot of money riding on his success.

Still, Junior has millions of fans pulling for him. A 2005 poll asked Americans to name their favorite sports stars. Dale Earnhardt, Jr., was the only race car driver to make the top ten. Fittingly, Number 8 ranked eighth in the poll.

A July victory in the USG Sheetrock 400 at Chicagoland Speedway in Illinois was one of Dale's few bright spots in 2005.

TIME LINE

1974 Ralph Dale Earnhardt, Jr., is born October 10 in Concord, North Carolina.

1996 Enters his first NASCAR Busch Series race.

1998 In his twentieth attempt, Dale Earnhardt, Sr., wins the Daytona 500. Dale Jr. claims his first Busch Series championship.

1999 Dale Jr. wins his second straight Busch Series title. He begins competing in NASCAR Winston Cup races.

2000 Gets his first Winston Cup win, in the DirecTV 500.

2001 Dale Sr. is killed in an accident in the final lap of the Daytona 500, while Dale Jr. finishes second.

2003 Dale Jr. finishes third in the Winston Cup point standings.

2004 Wins the Daytona 500. He suffers serious burns after crashing a Corvette in July.

2006 Dale Jr. finishes fifth in NASCAR Nextel Cup (formerly Winston Cup) points.

GLOSSARY

Busch Series — a NASCAR series that features shorter races and less powerful cars than the Nextel Cup. New drivers race in this series to gain experience.

late-model cars — automobiles that have been recently made.

NASCAR — short for the National Association for Stock Car Auto Racing.

Nextel Cup — the top NASCAR racing series, featuring the fastest cars and best drivers. It was previously called the Winston Cup.

pit stop — in auto racing, a stop during a race for fuel, fresh tires, and any repairs that are needed.

rookie — someone new to a job or activity, or in the first year as a pro in a sport.

rural — having to do with places away from cities, where fewer people live.

stock cars — the kind of race cars that compete in NASCAR events. At first, stock cars were ordinary, or stock, passenger cars. Today, the top stock cars are custom-built racing cars. Only their body shapes are similar to the everyday cars that people drive.

TO FIND OUT MORE

BOOKS

Dale Earnhardt, Jr. Sports Heroes and Legends (series). Matt Doeden (Lerner)

Dale Earnhardt Jr.: Born to Race. Sports Leaders (series). Ken Garfield (Enslow Publishers)

NASCAR. DK Eyewitness Books (series). James Buckley (DK Children)

VIDEOS

Dale Earnhardt Jr.: Any Given Day (NASCAR Images) NR

NASCAR: The IMAX Experience (Warner) PG

WEB SITES

Dale Earnhardt Inc.
www.daleearnhardtinc.com
The Earnhardt company's official site

NASCAR.com
www.nascar.com/
News and features at NASCAR's official site

Official Site of Dale Earnhardt, Jr.
www.dalejr.com
All about Junior, with sound and graphics

INDEX

About the Author

Geoffrey M. Horn has been a fan of music, movies, and sports for as long as he can remember. He has written more than two dozen books for young people and adults, along with hundreds of articles for encyclopedias and other works. He lives in southwestern Virginia, in the foothills of the Blue Ridge Mountains, with his wife, their collie, and four cats. He dedicates this book to his friends and neighbors in Franklin County, Virginia, where many racers got their start.